Dairy Group

by Megan Borgert-Spaniol

BLASTOFF!
2
READERS

BELLWETHER MEDIA • MINNEAPOLIS, MN

Note to Librarians, Teachers, and Parents:

Blastoff! Readers are carefully developed by literacy experts and combine standards-based content with developmentally appropriate text.

Level 1 provides the most support through repetition of high-frequency words, light text, predictable sentence patterns, and strong visual support.

Level 2 offers early readers a bit more challenge through varied simple sentences, increased text load, and less repetition of high-frequency words.

Level 3 advances early-fluent readers toward fluency through increased text and concept load, less reliance on visuals, longer sentences, and more literary language.

Level 4 builds reading stamina by providing more text per page, increased use of punctuation, greater variation in sentence patterns, and increasingly challenging vocabulary.

Level 5 encourages children to move from "learning to read" to "reading to learn" by providing even more text, varied writing styles, and less familiar topics.

Whichever book is right for your reader, Blastoff! Readers are the perfect books to build confidence and encourage a love of reading that will last a lifetime!

This edition first published in 2012 by Bellwether Media, Inc.

No part of this publication may be reproduced in whole or in part without written permission of the publisher. For information regarding permission, write to Bellwether Media, Inc., Attention: Permissions Department, 5357 Penn Avenue South, Minneapolis, MN 55419.

Library of Congress Cataloging-in-Publication Data

Borgert-Spaniol, Megan, 1989-
  Dairy group / by Megan Borgert-Spaniol.
    p. cm. – (Blastoff! readers. Eating right with myplate)
  Summary: "Relevant images match informative text in this introduction to the dairy group. Intended for students in kindergarten through third grade"– Provided by publisher.
  Includes bibliographical references and index.
  ISBN 978-1-60014-754-8 (hardcover : alk. paper)
  1. Nutrition–Juvenile literature. 2. Dairy products–Juvenile literature. I. Title.
  TX355.B647 2012
  641.3′7–dc23   2011033124

Printed in the United States of America, North Mankato, MN.

010112   1207

Contents

The Dairy Group

Dairy foods are an important part of a healthy meal.

The Dairy Group is made up of milk and foods made from milk.

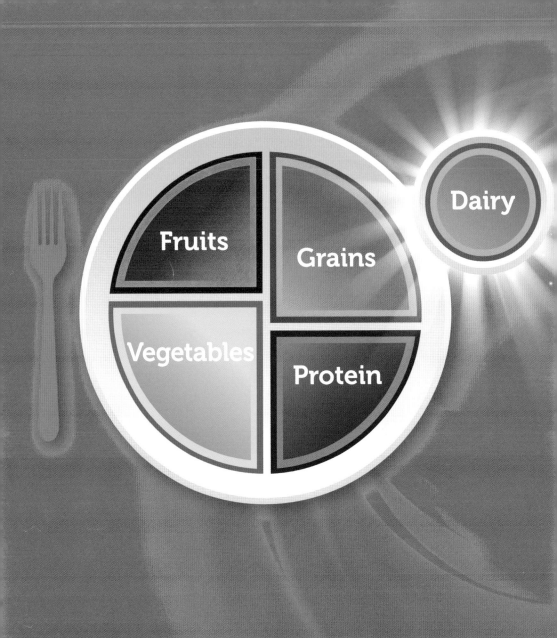

The Dairy Group is the blue part of **MyPlate**.

1 serving = 1 cup milk
2 cups cottage cheese
2 slices cheddar cheese
½ cup ricotta cheese
1 small container yogurt

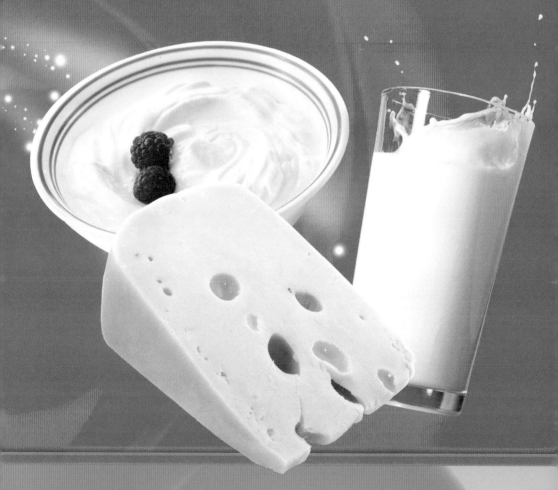

Kids should eat two and a half servings of dairy foods each day.

Why Are Dairy Foods Good For You?

Foods from the Dairy Group have **calcium** and **vitamin D**.

Calcium and vitamin D work together to build strong bones and teeth.

9

Dairy foods also have **potassium**.

Potassium keeps your muscles
healthy and gives you energy
to play.

Choosing Dairy Foods

You can drink milk with every meal. Choose skim or 1% milk.

Flavored milk has extra sugar in it. Plain milk is better for you.

Cheese and yogurt also
belong to the Dairy Group.

Choose cheese and yogurt with little or no **fat**.

Eating Dairy Foods

There are many ways to enjoy dairy foods. Mix yogurt with fruit or cereal for breakfast.

hard cheese

soft cheese

Eat **hard cheese** for a snack after school. Spread **soft cheese** on crackers or vegetables.

17

Pudding and ice cream are also dairy foods.

They are great treats after a healthy meal.

Dairy foods are important for growing kids.

20

Don't forget to put them on your plate!

Glossary

calcium—a part of some foods that your body needs to build strong bones and teeth

fat—a part of some foods that gives you energy and helps your body use vitamins; too much of certain fats is bad for your heart.

flavored—made with added sugar; chocolate milk and strawberry milk are flavored.

hard cheese—cheese that you can cut into slices; cheddar is a hard cheese.

MyPlate—a guide that shows the kinds and amounts of food you should eat each day

potassium—a part of some foods that keeps your muscles healthy and gives you energy

soft cheese—cheese that you can scoop or spread; cottage cheese is a soft cheese.

vitamin D—a part of some foods that helps your body use calcium

To Learn More

AT THE LIBRARY

Dickmann, Nancy. *Milk and Cheese*. Chicago, Ill.: Heinemann Library, 2011.

Parker, Victoria. *All About Dairy*. Irvine, Calif.: QEB Pub., 2009.

Rockwell, Lizzy. *Good Enough to Eat: A Kid's Guide to Food and Nutrition*. New York, N.Y.: HarperCollins Publishers, 1999.

ON THE WEB

Learning more about the Dairy Group is as easy as 1, 2, 3.

1. Go to www.factsurfer.com.

2. Enter "Dairy Group" into the search box.

3. Click the "Surf" button and you will see a list of related Web sites.

With factsurfer.com, finding more information is just a click away.

Index